ChAPTeRS

Tree-
HOUSE
comix
Proudly
Presents

DOG MAN
FeTCH-22

WRITTEN AND ILLUSTRATED BY **DAV PiLKeY**

AS GEORGE BEARD AND HAROLD HUTCHINS

WITH COLOR BY JOSE GARIBALDI

graphix

FOR MY EDITOR
AND FRIEND, KEN GEIST

Published in the UK by Scholastic Children's Books, 2020
Euston House, 24 Eversholt Street, London, NW1 1DB, UK
A division of Scholastic Limited.

First published in the US by Scholastic Inc., 2019

London – New York – Toronto – Sydney – Auckland
Mexico City – New Delhi – Hong Kong

ISBN 978 0702 30687 7

A CIP catalogue record for this book is available from the British Library.

The term "race car brain with bicycle brakes" on page 35 was coined by Dr. Edward
M. Hallowell, M.D., co-author of Delivered from Distraction: Getting the Most out
of Life with Attention Deficit Disorder.

Printed by Bell & Bain Limited, Glasgow
Papers used by Scholastic Children's Books are made
from wood grown in sustainable forests and other controlled sources.

1 3 5 7 9 10 8 6 4 2

www.scholastic.co.uk

INTRO #1

George AND HAROLD

The Men behind the Dog, Man!

Yo, SNOOPS!!! It's your old Buddies George and Harold!

'Sup?

We Just started 6th Grade a few months ago.

My, how Time Flies!

Now that we're **GROWN-UPS,** we've got some work to do!

So we're cleaning out our tree house.

TRASH

Yep! We're getting rid of all this **KID STUFF...**

TRASH

... To make room for **GROWN-UP STUFF!**

"When I was a child, I spoke like a child...

Goodbye, Super Diaper Baby comics.

...I thought like a child...

So long, Chubbs McSpiderbutt action figures and accessories.

...I reasoned like a child...

Farewell, homemade Pizza Box of Doom Playset.

INTRO #2 · DOG MAN

our Story thus Far:

One time a
cop and a
police dog...

...Got hurt in
an explosion!!!

KA-BLAM

They got rushed
to the Hospital...

wee-ooo-wee-ooo

...Where the Doctor
Gave them the
terrible news:

Boo
Hoo!

Dude! Your Head
is **DYING**!!!

Phooey!

And Doggy—Your body is dying!!!

whine whine

ALL Hope is Lost!!!

No it Ain't!

← Nurse Lady

Let's stitch the dog's head onto the cop's body!!!

Great idea, nurse lady!

And soon, an awesome new Hero was Born!!!

HOORAY FOR DOG MAN!!!

But then, things got complicated...

Petey the cat was busy living a life of wretchedness...

HAW HAW!

...when he accidentally created a kitty clone.

Papa?

Petey tried to make his little clone become evil...

...but it was not to be.

Kiss

Li'l Petey's kindness melted his Papa's heart...

... and now they are a family.

During the week, Li'l Petey lives with his Papa in a secret laboratory.

They build awesome robots together.

But on the weekends, Li'l Petey lives with his OTHER family.

80-HD: The world's most Remarkable Robot Buddy.

Their House.

Flip Flop Flip Flop Flip Flop Flip Flop

Together they play and make comics and stuff...

...but when help is needed, they transform into superheroes!!!

In our last adventure, Petey was reunited with his long-lost father.

It did not go well!

Petey's father stole all of their stuff...

...but he got busted by the cops.

Now he's in the slammer!

CHAPTER 1

THE FAIR FAIRY

By George Beard and Harold Hutchins

Dude, you went totally **<u>BONKERS!</u>**

That's not true, Downward Dog!

And don't call me "dude." We've talked about that!

I WAS THERE, Man! You FLIPPED OUT!!!

Now, now — I've already apologized for—

HEY, GARY! Roll that clip from last week!

<u>NO!</u>

22

28

CHAPTER 2

Shared Custody

By George Beard and Harold Hutchins

Soon...

Hey, fellas, it's almost five o'clock!

That means my Papa is gonna come over.

He's going to take me to his house for the week!

Remember our plan?

OK! Let's do it!!!

Well ya **CAN'T** bring them with you!!!

Rats!

NOW Let's GO!

Bye, fellas!

Hey, Papa...

...How come DoG Man and 80-HD Can't come and stay with us???

Because They **CAN'T!!!**

Why?

Look, I'm not trying to be mean...

...but Dog Man is a— he's just—

He'd lose his own **HEAD** if it wasn't sewn on!

And 80-HD is— he's just—

He's got a **RACE CAR BRAIN** with Bicycle **BRAKES!**

I just don't want those guys living in **OUR** house!!!

It's not fair!!!

Yeah, well, Life Ain't fair, kid. Get used to it!!!

poopy-doopy-stoopy-floopy

AND STOP THAT WHINING!!!

You're right, Papa.

I Am?

Yeah. I'm sorry.

I was **RiGhT** about Something?

CHAPTER 3

The Discovery

By George Beard and Harold Hutchins

The next day...

GASSY Behemoth TeLeVision

STUDIO A

Studio B

You wanted to see me, Larry?

MY NAME is SAM!

Whatever.

TAKE A CHAIR!!!

OK. I'll take this one.

HEY! Where Do yA Think you're Going?

YOU SAID I COULD T **SIT DOWN!**

I'm still keeping the chair, Larry!

Look—we've had **TONS** of complaints about your show!

You're mean to the children, You're rude to the staff...

FLIP

...You don't show up to work, You tell **LIES** CONSTANTLY...

FLIP FLIP

44

Meanwhile...

What'cha doing, kid?

I just made a discovery, Papa.

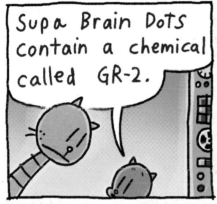

Supa Brain Dots contain a chemical called GR-2.

In high doses, it causes **SUPA ANGER!**

Look! This morning an **ANT** stole one of my Supa Brain Dots...

...and she started eating it.

First she Got Psychokinetic Brain Powers...

...and she started moving things with her mind.

Then came the SUPA Anger!

I drew these FLiP-O-Ramas to Show the progression!

INTRODUCING FLiP-O·

STEP 1.

First, place your Left hand inside the dotted Lines marked "Left hand here." Hold The book open FLAT!

STEP 2:

Grasp the right-hand Page with your Thumb and index finger (inside the dotted Lines marked "Right Thumb Here").

STEP 3:

Now QuickLy flip the right-hand page back and forth until the Picture appears to be Animated.

(for extra fun, try adding your own sound-effects!)

O-RAMA

REMEMBER,

While you are flipping, be sure you can see the image on page **49** **AND** the image on page **51**.

If you flip quickly, the two pictures will start to look like **ONE** **ANIMATED** cartoon.

Don't forget to add your own sound-effects!!!

Left hand here.

Stage 1
Anger

"Ant vs. Ant"

11:15 AM

Stage 2
Angrier

"Ant vs. Beetle"

11:17 Am

Stage 3
Supa Anger

"Ant vs. Kid with
Magnifying Glass"
11:30 Am

Right
Thumb
here.

But he's **CHANGED**, Papa. He's my friend now!

He's even in my comic club. See?

We make comics for each other every day!

I don't want you getting involved with that **CRAZY** fish!!!

It's too Late, Papa. I already sent my findings to Sarah!

She's gonna do a news story about it!

SLAP

ALRIGHT, LET'S GO!

Where?

I need you to hold the ladder for me.

Why?

Your Grampa stole the Letters from our sign...

...So I'm Gonna put some new Letters up!

Hey! What happened to Grampa?

But he's my Grampa!

HE BETRAYED YOU, TOO!

Trust me! That guy doesn't care about anybody but himself!

But Papa...

WE ARE NOT VISITING YOUR GRAMPA AND THAT IS FINAL!!!

CHAPTER 4

Visiting Grampa

By George Beard and Harold Hutchins

Hi! I'm Sarah Hatoff with Breaking News!

A DRUG company has recalled all Jars of SuPa Brain Dots ...

But don't worry, folks!

Right now, my most trusted officer...

...is going to every store in the city...

... and collecting all Jars of this dangerous drug!!!

58

With Dog Man in charge, what could possibly go wrong?

really?

Meanwhile...

Roxy's Pharmacy

open

Roxy's Pharmacy

Meanwhile...

It's so **UNFAIR!!!**

I can't believe Larry **FIRED** me!

I can!

He shoulda fired you a looooong time ago, dude!

NOBODY ASKED YOU, DOWNWARD DOG!!!

whatevs.

I **MUST** get my **REVENGE!!!**

65

---Twenty-one---
twenty-Two!!!

Sniff
Sniff

WAAAAAAAA!!!

Why are you
crying, Dude?

IT'S NOT FAIR!!!
ALL I ASked for was
A MiRACLe...

Sniff
Sniff

...but instead I got
Twenty-two baby
tadpoles who think
I'm their MOM!

AND STOP CALLING
ME "DUDE"!!!

Meanwhile...

CAT Jail →

I can't believe You talked me into visiting Your Grampa!!!

He's just going to betray us Again!

Maybe he will, Maybe he won't!

But don't You think we should give him another chance?

NO, I DON'T!

And So...

Oh, Gramps!!!

WHAT?!!?

HEY!!!
What's Going On?

Are you Concocting Some Sort of **Sleep GAS** or something?

Hi, Guys!

VISITING ROOM

I've missed you so much, son!

Yeah, **RIGHT!**

And I missed you most of all, Li'L Ralphie!

Li'L Petey!

Yeah! Li'L **PETEY!** That's what I SAID!

Look! I brought you a Present!

Thanks, Grampa!

And I even brought something for **ME!**

CHAPTER 5

TREE-
HOUSE
COMIX
Proudly
Presents

A Buncha Stuff That Happened Next

By George Beard 'N' Harold Hutchins

Welcome back to our news show!

And look who's here! It's **DOG MAN!**

He just finished collecting all of the **SUPA BRAiN DoTS** in the city!!!

Now nobody else will develop Psychokinetic Brain Powers...

...**OR** become Supa AnGry!

See? I **TOLD** ya nothing would go wrong!!!

Shake a paw, DOG Man!!!

HEY!!!

The WAGON iS ROLLING AWAY!

GeT it,
DOG MAN!

POW

PLip PLip PLiP PLop plip PLop Plippity PLop PLop plip PLop pli

Meanwhile...

cat Jail

Alrighty, then...

...The sleeping gas in the room has dissipated.

uu uu

Now it's time for Phase 2 of my evil plan!

SSSSSSSSHHHHHHH

SUPA SHAVE FOAM

SUPA SHAVE FOAM

SKRitcH SKRitcH

SKRitCH
SKRitch

TWING

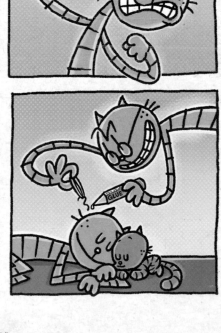

82

GLug GLug GLug

SQUIRCH

And now for the finishing touch!!!

Perfection!

But WAIT!

POP

Peeeel

ORANGE Juice

Okay, Sleepyhead! It's time to go!!!

84

And so...

85

91

Left hand here.

Right
Thumb
here.

Good! Now all we need is a name for this Tree Monster!

We must find a name that suggests **UNLIMITED POWER..**

...**UNSTOPPABLE EVIL...**

...**AND ULTIMATE DESTRUCTION!!!**

A name that will strike terror into the hearts of **ALL!**

I'VE GOT it!

CHAPTER 6
BARKY McTreeFace

We Are **NOT** Calling him "Barky McTreeface"!

Aw, come on, dude! That's a <u>COOL</u> Name!

THAT'S the **DUMBEST** NAME I EVER HEARD!

Well I Like it.

So do I!!!

We **LOVE** Barky McTreeface!!!!

Hey, Let's make up a Song about him!

Yeah!

OK!

Good idea!

YOU BETTER NOT!

Down to the city...

...causing Cataclysmic crime...

Punching here and there...

... Smashing everywhere...

... Now it's **FLIP-O-RAMA** Time!

DO IT!!!

Left hand here.

Right
Thumb
her

Flippity Flip-Flip
Slappity-slap.
Look at Barky Punch!
Flippity Flip-flip
Kickety-Kick.
He'll eat ya up for Lunch!

Haw Haw Haw! Look at that **DESTRUCTION!**

Now things Are becoming **FAIR!**

Wait a minute— How does **THIS** Make things Fair?

I Just lost my **JOB!** I Lost **EVERYTHING!**

Yeah. So?

So now I'm taking **EVERYTHING** Away from **EVERYONE** else!

109

Meanwhile...

HEY!!!

WHAT'S the big idea?

You fell asleep, Grampa!

GRAMPA?

I'm **NOT GRAMPA!** I'm **PETEY!!!!!**

Yeah, but what about your tail and whiskers???

That's just **GLUE** and **MARKERS** and stuff!!!

Sorry, Grampa! I'm not falling for your tricks AGain!

WAit A minute—I've Gotta find my SON!

Oh, don't worry about him...

...Petey left here about an hour ago.

He had your little Grandson with him!

LOOK-You've got to Listen to Me!

THAT KID is iN TERRiBLE DANGER! LET Me OUT oF HERE NOW!!!

Hi, Grampa!

Okay.

Hey, I'm Hungry!

Well go cook some food then, ya freeloader!

What do I look like? Your **SERVANT?**

My Papa always cooks for me.

You **DID** say you were my Papa, didn't you?

SLAP!

And so...

CHAPTER 7

FLiPPY ReTurns

Meanwhile...

FiSH JaiL

FiSh JaiL

Haw Haw Haw Haw!

ish aiL

MY eviL PLan is WORKiNG!!!!!!!

Soon I Shall take over the WorLd!!!

But first, I must destroy that Robo-cat!

HAW HAW HAW

HAW HAW HAW

What happened next, Flippy?

Well, Let's turn the page and find out!!!

FLIP

Suddenly...

CRASH!

The End. MY STORY by FLIPPY

...The Robo-cat was in my Grasp!!!

"The end."

"Hooray!" "Awesome!" "Sweeet!"

CAT KID'S COMIC CLUB

"YAY!" "Bravo!!!" "Thanks, everyone!!!"

But then...

"Hey, FLippy! the Mayor's on the phone!"

"Hello?"

"Pack your bags, FLippy! You're a FREE Fish!"

"I am?"

"Yep! Li'L Petey's Research Proved you were innocent!!!"

I'm Free!

Congratulations, FLIPPY!!!

Let's Go Fill out the Paperwork...

...And Soon, all your problems will be over!

We interrupt this chapter with a tragic update:

BREAKING NEWS

A Giant tree is attacking the city...

POW!

LIVE

...And it looks like it's being Controlled by...

LIVE

...well, uh...

...MISTAKES WERE MADE!!!

But don't worry, Folks! I've put Dog Man in charge...

...of fetching those twenty-two tiny Tadpoles!!!

Once he fetches them...

...we'll get them the help they need!

CHAPTER 8

Tree-House Comix Proudly Presents

The Fetcher in the SKY

GEORGE HAROLD

But then...

We interrupt this tenderhearted moment with Breaking News:

Dog Man and chief are heading to town...

...to stop the evil tree that is ATTACKING the city!

Evil Tree? Attacking the city?

This looks like a job for COMMANDER CUPCAKE!!!

Huff Puff Huff

Huff
Puff
Puff

Puff
Puff
huff

huff Puff

Um— what are you doing?

Well you see, Grampa...

...I'm not like other cats.

...And I champion the cause of carbohydrates!

Amen!

NOBODY CARES!!!

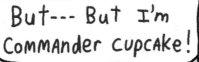

But--- But I'm Commander Cupcake!

WELL THAT'S JUST GREAT!

I was just thinking: What we **REALLY NEED** Right Now...

...is A Guy in a Cape whose **ONLY** Superpower is that he eats a lot of **CUPCAKES!!!**

I also eat sprinkles!

THAT'S NOT HELPFUL!!!

We're stuck in here without A key!!!

Psst! We don't need a key, Grampa!

We shall escape through my Cupcake Corridor!

Watch this!

BONK!

HANG IN THERE!!!

HANG IN THERE!!!

YOU HAD AN ESCAPE TUNNEL THIS WHOLE TIME...

...AND YOU DIDN'T TELL ME??

You didn't ask!

Meanwhile...

As Dog Man and his friends got closer to the scene of the crime...

NETS

... they Grabbed some weapons...

... and Prepared for an epic Battle!!!

It's time to give up, Fair Fairy!!!

NEVER!!! You **DO-GOODERS** Can't stop my **SUPA-AnGry PSYCHOKineTic TADPoLes!**

STOP The TADpoles, DoG Man!!!

STOP The Dog Man, Tadpoles!!!

And so...

SWISH

145

Left hand here.

Right
Thumb
here.

PETEY
&
SON

You did, too!!!

I DID **NOT**!

Oh, hi, Zuzu!

Screech

BARK BARK BARK!!!

What's that you say? Dog Man's in trouble?

RUFF RUFF BARK BARK BARK!

Sarah and Chief, too?

80-HD, Don't FAIL Me NOW!

ZOOOOOM

156

Meanwhile...

Well, here we are at last, Grampa...

...MY Cupcake Command Center.™

Let's check the cupcake computer!

Look, we haven't got time for this!

I've gotta go and save my SON!!!

But you haven't seen the cupcake cabana yet...

...or the cupcake croquet court...

...or the—

I JUST WANNA SEE The CUPCAKE EXIT!!!

Well why didn't you say so???

SLAP

Hey!

I think your back got stuck on my hand somehow!!!

OH, well — come on, Grampa!

CHAPTER 10
MY FAIR LADY

Hello again, folks! I'm Sarah Hatoff Reporting from...

.. a floating net.

We've all been captured by twenty-two Supa-angry psychokinetic tadpoles...

...And they're holding us in the sky with their Brain Powers.

How will we ever get out of this mess???

BUMP BINK BOMP

Gee, that was a lot easier than I thought it would be!!!

And Look, FLippy the bionic Butterfly fish...

...has joined our fight for **GOOD!**

But there's only four of us!!!

And twenty-five of us!!!

How will we ever get out of <u>this</u> mess?

Never fear, Sarah!!!

ZIP

IT'S SUPA BUDDY TIME!

COSTUMES

167

Indeed she was Right. The Supa Buddies and their friends...

...had Given their all...

... and had put up a valiant Fight.

(GOOD VIBES)

But they were outnumbered...

CRASH!

... outmatched...

PUNT

... and out of time!

YOINK

One by one, our heroes were captured...

...And the powers of evil grew stronger and stronger.

BARK BARK BARK

Ruff Ruff Ruff

Look at me!!! I'm **FLYING**, BABY!

CHAPTER 11

The Cat Kid Conundrum

174

Ready to slice.

And in this perfect moment...

...When a swipe from his sharpened sabers...

...Promises sweet salvation...

...he stops.

ShinG

What's your name?

Molly.

Oh. I'm Li'l Petey.

Hey, guess what? I have a comic club!

You do?

Yeah. You can join if you want to.

But I never made a comic before.

It's okay.

I can show ya how. It's <u>FUN</u>!!!

You'll teach me?

of course.

That's what friends do. They help each other.

As the two friends talked and laughed, Something started to change in Molly...

Ha Ha Ha

Ha Ha Ha

...and soon, her Supa Anger began melting away.

WHAT'S GOING ON HERE?!!?

CHAPTER 12

Good Golly Miss Molly

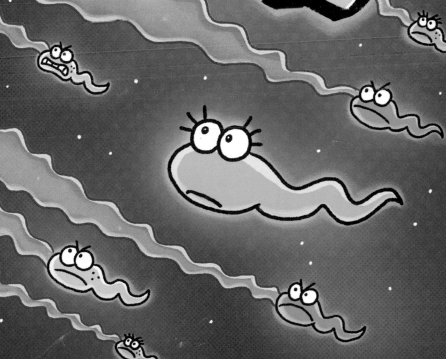

It is easy to join with the crowd...

...and even easier to spread anger and hate.

But it takes courage to stand alone.

And kindness often takes the most courage of all.

Molly could not move the mighty tree all by herself...

... but she could move a branch...

C-C-CREAK!

... and that was all she needed.

C'mon, gang! I've got an idea!!!

They're Getting Away!!!

Aw, Let 'em Go!

What could one tiny tadpole and one tiny kitten and one tiny poodle possibly do?

DUDE— seriously?

Hey, what's up, 'Puter?

'Sup?

supa 'puter

We need your help, brah!

'K

We need to create an **ANTiDOTE** to Supa Brain DoTs.

No prob. I'll download the components...

...then calculate a recipe for our concoction using everyday ingredients.

Sweeet!

C'mon, gang! Let's go find some everyday ingredients!!!

And soon...

Ok, what next?

...now add two teaspoons of ketchup...

... and a dash of paprika...

SHaka Shaka Shake

'puter

Lastly, pour the mixture into my subcritical fission reactor.

One Nuclear trans-mutation Later...

DinG ♪

supa 'puter

CHAPTER 13

THE FINAL BETRAYAL

Soon...

Hi, Papa!

Where have **YOU** been?

Those Tadpoles are almost done destroying your friends!

We were making an **ANTIDOTE!!!**

It's in this balloon!

All we have to do is Pop it...

...and those tadpoles will all Lose their SuPA Powers!!!!!

You better go hide in that swamp now, Molly...

...and stay under the water so ya won't breathe the antidote!

That way You won't Lose **Your** Supa Powers!!!

Okay! See ya Later!!!

OK, TADPOLES— LISTEN UP !!!!

I want you all to hide in that SWAMP over there!

Stay underwater, and don't breathe the air for a few minutes!!!

OK, Mommy!

See ya Later!

Bye, Mom!

Mean-while...

You'd better wipe that **SMILE** off of Your face, Young Lady...

...because things are about to Get **SERIOUS**!!!

He's Gonna Pop that balloon and...

...and...

KLUNK

W-What Happened???

LOOK!

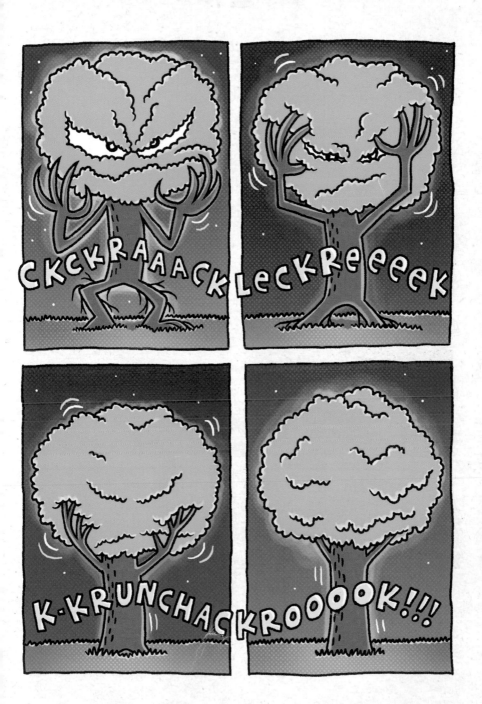

THAT ANTIDOTE RUINED EVERYTHING!

Hey, wait a minute!

There's No Antidote in this balloon, is there???

Nope.

YOU LiED TO ME!!! YOU BETRAYED ME!!

I guess I did...

... GRAMPA!

Zuzu's the real hero Today!!!

She poured the antidote into the swamp and saved the world!!!

HOORAY FOR ZUZU!!!

whisper whisper whisper

204

HEY, LOOK! Commander Cupcake did it **AGAIN!**

He captured the fair fairy _AND_ Grampa!!!

You two criminals are going to **JAIL!**

NOT SO FAST!

This isn't Grampa! This is my Papa!

But he looks Just Like Grampa!!!

Show 'em, 80-HD!!!

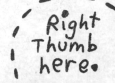

Gentle
Rinse

Delicate
cleanse

Relaxing
Blow
Dry

Do Good, Flippy

215

Where, Flippy?

Well, there are twenty-one baby tadpoles in that swamp back there...

...and I'll bet they're feeling pretty lonely and afraid all by themselves.

I remember how that felt.

So I was thinking...

... maybe they could use a friend.

You were so Good to me when I was in fish JaiL, L.P.

You made comics for me every day!

You inspired me! You Kept me Going!

Now it's my turn to **DO GOOD!**

Hey! I wanna Do Good, too!!!

Well You can help me if ya want!

Okay!

And You Guys can visit us at the swamp anytime!!!

Yeah! You still have to teach me how to make comics!

I will!

Maybe You can teach all twenty-two of us!

Okay!

Well, let's go, Kiddo!

Bye, Li'l Petey!

Bye, old Guy!

All he's really doing is looking after a few baby tadpoles.

That's not really gonna change the world!

Maybe not...

...but it'll change their world!

SARAH HAT OFF
NEWS BLOG WITH SARAH HATOFF

FORMER FISH FELON FINDS FAMILY

Flippy the bionic psychokinetic butterfly fish was released from fish jail last week, and is already making an impact in our community. In this exclusive interview, Flippy shares his inspiring story:

Q. How has life changed since you were in Fish Jail?
A. WELL, I MOVED INTO A SWAMP AND NOW I'M RAISING A BUNCH OF BABY TADPOLES.

Q. How did you meet them?
A. WE MET LAST WEEK WHEN THEY TRIED TO DESTROY THE PLANET.

Q. Weren't you afraid of them?
A. NAH. I KNEW THEY WERE GOOD KIDS DEEP DOWN INSIDE. AND I WAS RIGHT.

Q. Were they happy to see you?
A. THEY DIDN'T RECOGNIZE ME. THEY HAD NO MEMORY OF THEIR TERRIFYING ORDEAL. IN FACT, THEY ALL STARTED CALLING ME "DADDY."

Menu ☰

Q. So what did you do?
A. I HAD NO CHOICE. I ADOPTED THEM ALL.
Q. So what's next for you and your new family?
A. RIGHT NOW I'M TEACHING EVERYBODY TO
READ AND WRITE. MY FRIEND MOLLY IS
HELPING, AND CAT KID IS TEACHING US ALL
HOW TO MAKE OUR OWN COMICS!

CAT KID'S COMIC CLUB!

Local kitten Li'l Petey has started his own comic club,
and it's gaining new members every day. If you would like
to start your OWN chapter of Cat Kid's Comic Club, go to
scholastic.com/catkidclub to download everything you
need. It's free and it's FUN!

DOG MAN IS GO!

An ALL-NEW Dog Man novel is coming SOON, and it's
going to be the BEST ONE YET!!! The title of the all-
graphic novel is going to be DOG MAN
d it will be available next sum

NOTES

by George and Harold

⭐ On pages 6 and 7, George is adapting a well-known quote from the Bible. (1 Corinthians 13:11 (KJV & NLT).)

⭐ Petey's rant on page 36–38 was inspired by the following quote:

> "Life is never fair ... And perhaps
> it is a good thing for most of us
> that it is not." — Oscar Wilde

⭐ The Barky McTreeface song (Chapter 6) can be sung to the tune of any magical snowman-themed song you can think of.

⭐ The final chapter was inspired by The Star Thrower by Loren Eiseley, as well as Joel Barker's adaptation. It goes kinda like this:

> A guy walking along the seashore
> saw a kid picking up starfish from the sand
> and gently throwing them back into the ocean.
> "Whatcha doing?" asked the guy.
> "These starfish were washed ashore," said the kid,
> "and they will die if they don't get back to the sea."
> "But there are thousands of starfish along this shore,"
> said the guy. "You can't possibly make a difference."
> The kid gently threw another starfish out into the sea.
> "I made a difference to that one," she said.

HOW 2 DRAW DOG MAN

in **29** Ridiculously easy steps!

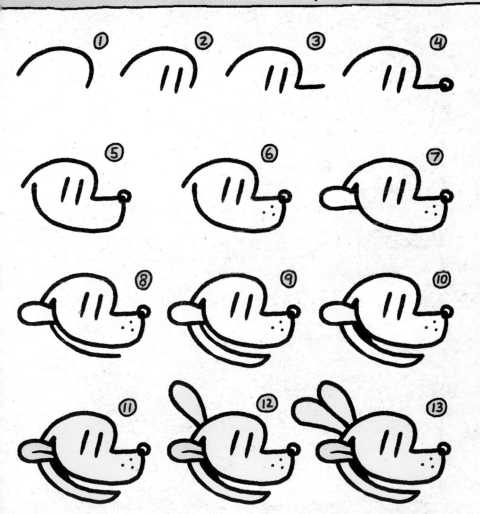

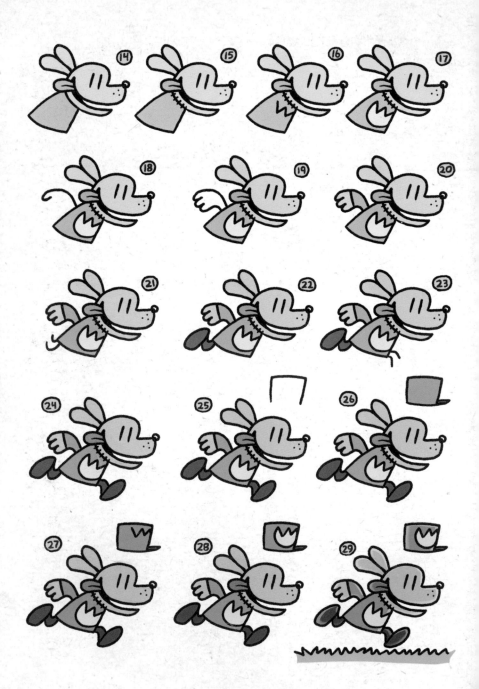

HOW 2 DRAW Li'L PeTeY

in 21 Ridiculously Easy steps!

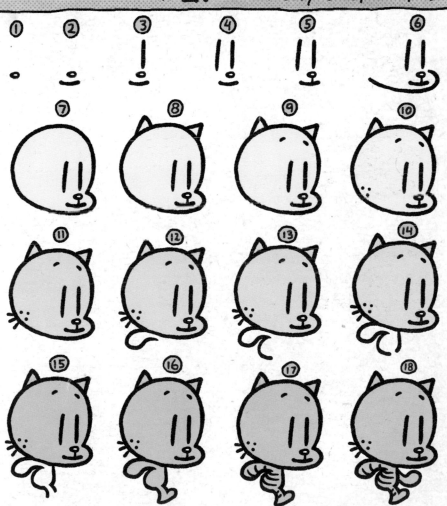

HOW 2 DRAW MOLLY

in 9 Ridiculously Easy Steps!

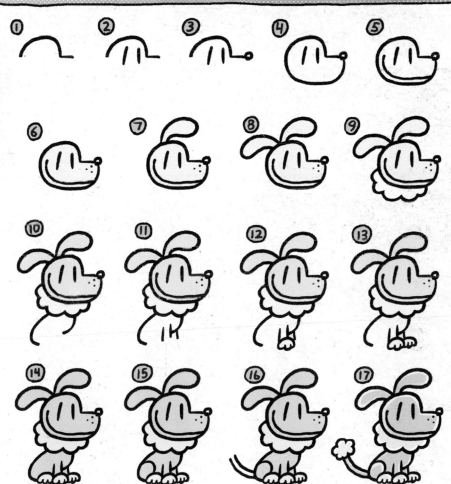

HOW 2 DRAW Mc BARKY TREEFACE

in 24 Ridiculously Easy Steps!

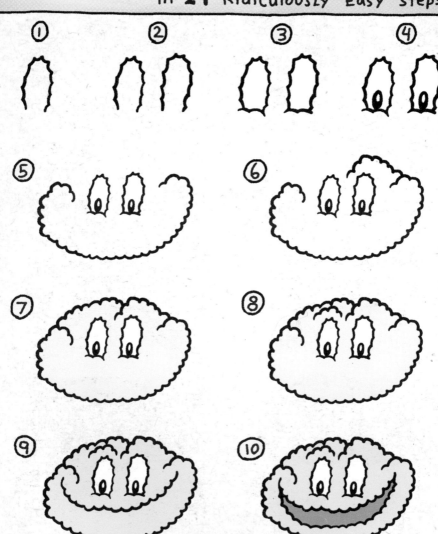

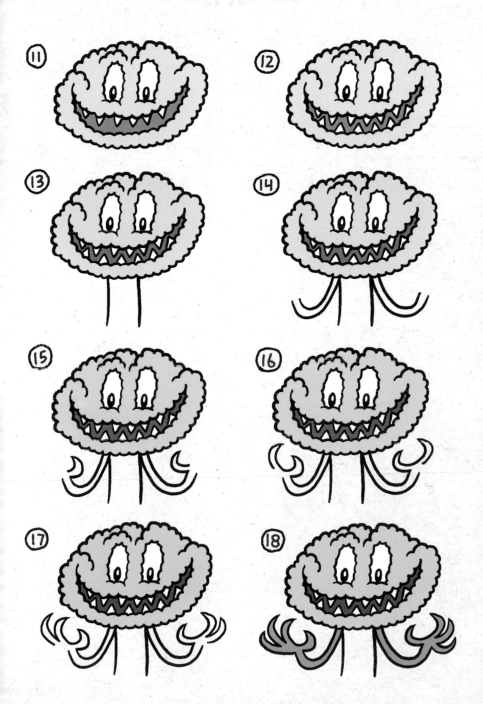

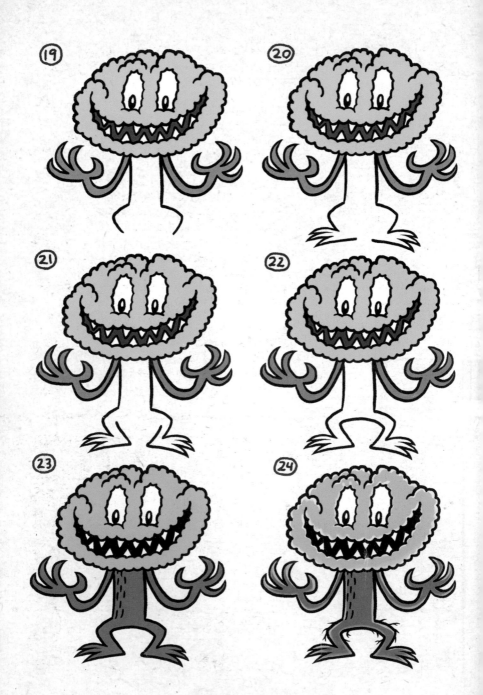

BONUS!

NOW YOU CAN SING THE FINAL VERSES OF BARKY'S SONG!

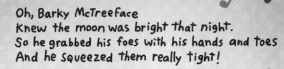

Oh, Barky McTreeface
Knew the moon was bright that night.
So he grabbed his foes with his hands and toes
And he squeezed them really tight!

Then all the tadpoles
flew into a swampy bay.
And the medicine Zuzu poured Right in
Made their powers go away!

So Barky dropped our heroes
and he turned back to a tree.
Then the bad guys went to jail and
that's the end of our story.

Now Barky McTreeface
is so peaceful, calm, and zen.
And if you do good like ya Know you should
then he won't come back again!!!

Peace-ity peace-peace, zen-ity zen
Look at Barky now!
Do-ity Do-Do, Good-ity Good
He won't come back No-how!!!

YOU BETTER NOT!

OLD LAdy Jail

GET READING W

TH DAV PILKEY!

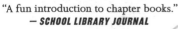

ABOUT THE AUTHOR-ILLUSTRATOR

When Dav Pilkey was a kid, he was diagnosed with ADHD and dyslexia. Dav was so disruptive in class that his teachers made him sit out in the hall every day. Luckily, Dav loved to draw and make up stories. He spent his time in the hallway creating his own original comic books.

In the second grade, Dav Pilkey made a comic book about a superhero named Captain Underpants. Since then, he has been creating books that explore fun, positive themes and inspire readers everywhere.

ABOUT THE COLORIST

Jose Garibaldi grew up on the South Side of Chicago. As a kid, he was a daydreamer and a doodler, and now it's his full-time job to do both. Jose is a professional illustrator, painter, and cartoonist who has created work for many organizations, including Nickelodeon, MAD Magazine, Cartoon Network, Disney, and THE EPIC ADVENTURES OF CAPTAIN UNDERPANTS for DreamWorks Animation. He lives in Los Angeles, California, with his wonder dogs, Herman and Spanky.